STEP-UP
GEOGRAPHY

Should the high street be closed to traffic?

Julia Roche

Evans

Published by Evans Brothers Limited
2A Portman Mansions
Chiltern Street
London W1U 6NR

© Evans Brothers Limited 2005

Produced for Evans Brothers Limited by
White-Thomson Publishing Ltd,
Bridgewater Business Centre,
210 High Street,
Lewes, East Sussex BN7 2NH

Printed in China by New Era Printing Co. Ltd

Project manager: Ruth Nason

Designer: Helen Nelson, Jet the Dog

Consultant: John Lace, School Improvement
Manager, Hampshire County Council

Cover: All photographs by Chris Fairclough

British Library Cataloguing in Publication Data

Roche, Julia

Should the high street be closed to traffic?. - (Step-
up geography)
1.Pedestrian area - Juvenile literature 2.Urban
transportation - Enviromental aspects - Juvenile
literature 3.City planning - Environmental aspects
- Juvenile literature

I. Title

388.4'1

ISBN: 0 237 528770

Picture acknowledgements:

Corbis: page 25b (London Aerial Photo Library);
Docklands Light Railway: page 15l; Ecoscene:
page 11l (Angela Hampton); Chris Fairclough
Photo Library: pages 4t, 5b, 11cl, 11b, 12t, 12b,
16bl, 20t; London Transport: page 15r;
Michael Nason: pages 18t, 18tr, 19tr, 22r, 22b;
White-Thomson Photo Library: pages 1, 13c, 13b,
17br. All other photographs are by Chris
Fairclough.

Contents

The high street

Almost every town has a busy high street. What are the differences and the similarities between the high streets shown here and the main shopping street in your town?

People visit the high street for many reasons. Some work there, for example in shops, offices and banks. Some go to shop or just to relax. What places are there in your high street where people can go to meet friends? Are there any places where people go for entertainment, such as cinemas, theatres or bingo halls?

On some high streets there are buildings for the community, such as schools, libraries and sports centres. Most high streets also have places of worship, such as churches, mosques and synagogues.

▲ *What reasons might these people have for visiting their high street?*

▶ *In your high street are there some banks, a place of worship, and a town hall?*

▶ *Are any shops in this picture the same as in your high street? Many towns have shops that are branches of big chain stores.*

High street homes

Some people live in the high street, either in houses or in flats above shops. Living in the town centre is convenient, but it does not suit everyone. Can you think of reasons why?

There are not many homes in the high street. There is more space away from the town centre for blocks of flats and houses with gardens, and so the residential areas are often on the outskirts of the town. Housing there may be cheaper than in the high street.

Traffic in the high street

All the vehicles that bring workers, shoppers and other high street users into the town centre are called local traffic. There is also through traffic – vehicles on their way to somewhere else.

▲ *This high street in South London is part of the A24, a main road linking other towns. It is therefore full of traffic. Is your high street part of a main road?*

Your high street

Try looking at your high street on a map. You might spot things you did not know were there. An Ordnance Survey (OS) map shows a very detailed view, or your local tourist board may have a map like this one of Kendal.

The high street in Kendal is called Highgate. What is your high street called? What information to help visitors would you include on a map of your high street?

▶ *This map shows the main street of Kendal, in Cumbria. Can you use it to give someone directions from the bus station to the cinema?*

Key

	Shops		Place of worship
	Pedestrian precinct		Coach drop-off point
P	Car park	- - -	Cycle path
→	One-way traffic	①	Bus station
i	Tourist information office	②	Library
PO	Post office	③	Council offices
††	Toilets	④	Cinema
⚏	Children's play area	⑤	Museum

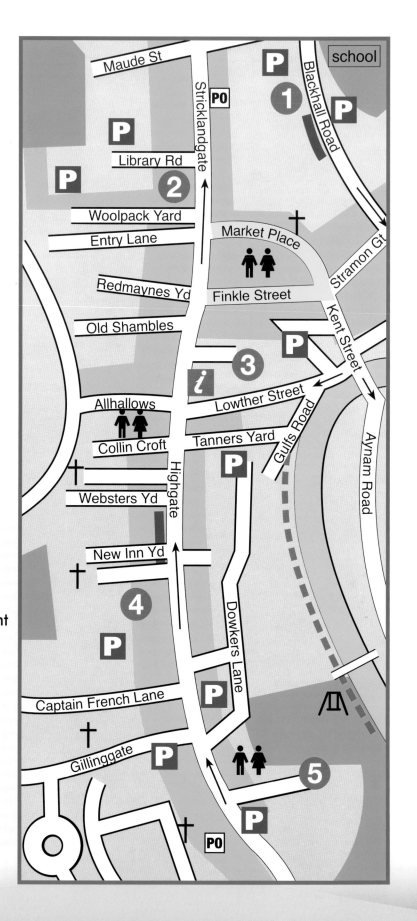

Changes

High streets change over the years. Most of the buildings are rented out on a lease. The lease says what the building can be used for – whether it can be a restaurant, shop or office, for example. Perhaps you can remember what some of the buildings in your high street used to be? Your library might have local history books with old photos of your town, showing what shops were there long ago.

▶ *This charity shop has been open for a year. Before that, it was a bookshop.*

▼ *How many kinds of surface can you find on the ground in your high street? You might spot paving stones, tarmac on the road and concrete gutters. Some parts of the pavement have a raised pattern, for example near pedestrian crossings. Who do you think these tactile surfaces help?*

Sound levels

You could use a sound meter to gather information about the levels of noise at different spots along your high street. Plot the readings on a graph, with decibels on one axis and areas of the high street on the other.

Decibels

7

Traffic and pedestrians

Perhaps you could do a traffic survey to find out about the volume of traffic in your high street. You would need to watch for different types of vehicles, such as bikes, cars, buses, vans and heavy goods vehicles (HGVs), and record how many of each type you see.

▼ *Use a tally sheet to record how many vehicles you see.*

▲ *Which types of vehicle are in this high street? If you surveyed your high street, which types of vehicle would you count?*

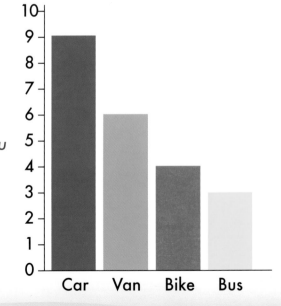

▶ *Use the data from your tally sheet to make a pictogram.*

Think about what you would find if you surveyed the traffic at different times of day. How would your pictograms be different?

Pedestrians

All drivers and their passengers will, at some time, become pedestrians and walk on the pavements. The word 'pedestrian' comes from the Latin word *pedes*, meaning 'feet'. Pavements are also used by people with wheelchairs or electrically powered scooters.

Things that help

All high streets are different, but every high street has things that have been put there to help both traffic and pedestrians to move easily and stay safe. Some examples are:

- traffic lights
- central refuges
- footbridges
- pedestrian-only areas
- yellow lines (double or single)
- pelican crossings
- underpasses
- speed bumps
- roundabouts.

Do these things help pedestrians or traffic or both? Try making a table to record your ideas.

◀ *Are the people on this high street using the crossing safely?*

Your high street

Look carefully at what is in your high street to help the people who use it. Try making a simple map of your high street, using symbols to show things that help. Remember to make a key for your map.

Some symbols for your map

- traffic lights
- underpass
- central refuge
- pelican or zebra crossing
- speed bumps
- footbridge
- roundabout

Traffic problems

More and more people are using cars these days. Everyone has their own point of view about the problems extra traffic can cause.

Here are six photos of people who have made comments about traffic problems in their high street. Can you match one comment to each picture?

Delivery van driver

Car driver

I get fed up sitting in traffic jams. It's difficult to find a space to park, too.

I wear a mask so I don't breathe in the traffic fumes. Sometimes cars come very close to me.

I wish car drivers would stay out of the bus lane. It's so annoying.

I worry about the smelly fumes and all the noise, especially for my children.

The pavements are so crowded. There aren't enough safe places to cross, either.

Often there are cars in the way, or double yellow lines, where I want to stop to make a delivery.

Cyclist

Bus driver

Pedestrian

Parent

Your own high street

Could any of these comments be about your high street? With a friend, try listing some local traffic problems. Give each problem a mark out of five, depending on how serious you think it is:

1 A bit inconvenient

2 Quite annoying

3 Really annoying

4 Could be dangerous

5 Seriously dangerous

With your friend, discuss ways of solving the traffic problems, starting with the most serious ones. Then share your ideas with the whole class.

A traffic rap

Write a rap to sum up the traffic problems in your high street. It could start:

Let me tell you about the problems in my high street

With all the traffic jams and fumes, it doesn't smell sweet…

Solving traffic problems

Changes can be made to pavements and roads in order to reduce traffic problems. Problems are also reduced if all road users follow the Highway Code.

Safer pavements

Where pavements are crowded and pedestrians and traffic come dangerously close, some solutions are:

- Widen the pavement. (What happens to the road width?)
- Add railings to separate traffic and pedestrians.
- Put bollards at intervals along the kerb to stop vehicles mounting the pavement.

The Highway Code

Find a copy of the Highway Code and read the Rules for Pedestrians, especially The Green Cross Code. If you are allowed to cycle on the roads, read the Rules for Cyclists. Also find out if you could take part in a Cycling Proficiency course.

◀ The railings in this high street help to ensure that pedestrians only cross at the pelican crossing. However, some people believe that railings spoil the appearance of the street.

Adding places to cross

How many kinds of crossing can you list? There are some examples on pages 8-9. Do you know the differences between zebra, pelican, toucan and puffin crossings? The Highway Code will tell you.

When a council wants to make a new crossing, they must decide which kind and where. If the high street is wide and traffic is heavy, a footbridge or underpass might be suitable – but these may be expensive to build and spoil the appearance of the high street. A crossing must be positioned where people want to cross and where it is safe for traffic to stop.

◀ At a pelican crossing, green lights and a bleeping sound tell people when it is safe to cross.

◀ A dropped kerb is helpful for many pedestrians.

Improving traffic flow

Ways of reducing traffic jams in the high street include:

- Create bus lanes and bicycle lanes.
- Build roundabouts at road junctions.
- Create a one-way system.
- Provide clear traffic signs.
- Do not allow parking on the roadside.

▶ A bus lane allows buses to move freely, out of the way of cars.

Transport for the future

Every year the number of cars increases, so traffic problems are likely to become worse. We can try to avoid that by making changes.

Cleaner vehicles

Many people are working to solve the problem of fumes from petrol- and diesel-powered vehicles, which pollute the air and harm our health and the environment. Scientists are investigating how to produce cleaner fuels, and engineers are developing engines that use fuel more efficiently. Manufacturers are looking at ways of improving and developing vehicles powered by electricity and smaller cars such as Smart cars, which use less fuel.

▶ *Most car drivers today fill their petrol tanks with lead-free petrol, which is an improvement on what was available in the past.*

By 2030 we may be able to use a new fuel developed from methane hydrates. There are vast quantities of this material buried under the seas, and it burns more cleanly than oil or coal. However, bringing it to the surface could create more environmental problems than it solves. For example, parts of the Arctic ice cap could be destroyed, harming plant and animal life.

◀ *Smart cars are designed for driving in town, because they can be parked in small spaces.*

Public transport

Traffic problems can be reduced if people use public transport instead of cars. How often do you travel by bus, train or tram? Why do you use these forms of transport? How would you encourage people to use public transport instead of travelling to places by car?

Why people don't use public transport

- Long waits
- Trains and buses often late
- Expensive
- Uncomfortable and crowded
- Have to change from one bus/train to another

Ways to improve public transport

- More frequent and reliable
- Easier access for people with luggage, pushchairs, or wheelchairs
- Cheaper fares
- More direct routes

◀ Many people benefit when buses and trains are made easier to get into and out of.

▶ At this bus stop, information can be seen and heard about when the buses will be arriving.

A pedestrian precinct

A pedestrian precinct is an area reserved for pedestrians only, at least during the busiest shopping times.

Pedestrian Zone Ahead No access to Town Centre

In a pedestrian precinct people can enjoy being in the high street without having to worry about the dangers of traffic.

They can sit with their friends and children at the pavement cafés and enjoy some street entertainment, such as musicians and dancers, as they relax after shopping or work.

Health benefits

Users of a pedestrianised high street benefit from cleaner air, free from traffic fumes. People who would normally drive to the high street find other ways to get there. They may park further out of town and walk or catch a bus to the high street. Walking is an excellent choice as it helps with fitness and can help to prevent obesity and heart disease.

Some disadvantages

There will never be one solution to any problem that suits everyone. Can you think of high street users who might not like the idea of the high street being closed to traffic? Discuss with your family and friends some of the disadvantages for:

- shopkeepers – e.g. they may lose business;

- shoppers – e.g. they have to park further from the shops, and there is less feeling of community in the high street as people choose to shop elsewhere;

- delivery drivers – e.g. they have to make deliveries outside normal business hours.

PEDESTRIAN ZONE

No vehicles

Except for loading
Midnight - 10am
4 pm - Midnight
Permit holders
and taxis

At any time

◀ *Between which times are delivery vans and lorries allowed to drive into this pedestrian area for 'loading'?*

Role play

In a group, prepare some role play of different high street users and some of their comments after traffic has been banned.

▲ ◀ *Many high street shopkeepers worry that they are losing customers, because people prefer to drive to out-of-town shopping centres, or to order goods by phone or internet, for delivery to their homes.*

Designing a precinct

As well as being safer and pollution-free, a precinct can be a beautiful and pleasant place. It can have landscaped areas, with sculptures and artwork by local artists, including children.

Are there special features in your high street, like a fountain or a statue of a local person, which could be used in a pedestrian precinct to make it a place to be proud of?

Make sketches of some interesting street furniture in your town. The pictures on this page show some examples.

You might also carry out a survey among your family and friends to find out what they would like in a pedestrian precinct. You could start the list with:

- pleasant seating areas;
- clean and easily accessible toilets with baby-changing facilities;
- lots of well-designed litter bins.

If some of your friends do the same, you could record all your results as a table on the computer. You could do a survey on a larger scale by asking your local library if you may put a suggestions box there for anyone to give their ideas. How would you make your suggestions box eye-catching?

A dream precinct

Use mapping software to create a picture of a 'dream precinct' with hotspots for annotated features.

Some other things to consider when designing a pedestrian precinct are:

- styles of signposting;
- street lighting;
- road and pavement surfaces.

▲ *What properties do you think road and pavement surfaces should have?*

What might spoil the area?

Litter and graffiti are unsightly and spoil otherwise pleasant areas. Litter can be dangerous, causing people to slip. Food litter attracts rats, which spread disease. Litter is cleared by street cleaners, but these valuable workers have to be paid. Your local council pays them using money, called council tax, which is collected from all local residents. If there was less litter, less council tax could be used for street cleaning and more could be spent on providing other things for the community.

19

Making the precinct accessible

Town planners must consider the needs of all the different people who will visit a new pedestrian precinct. The precinct must be accessible for everyone.

People will come to the edge of the precinct on foot, by bicycle, car or other private vehicle, or by bus, tram or train. There must be safe and convenient paths into the precinct from car parks, bus and tram stops and railway stations. These paths need to be clearly signposted.

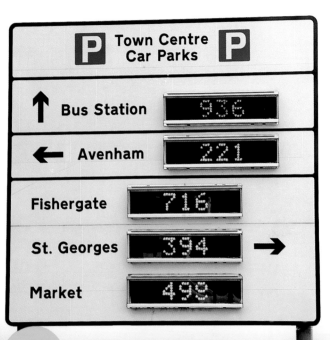

▲ *Trams are a cleaner form of transport than buses. They run on rails set into the road and are powered by electricity from overhead cables.*

◄ *Clear signposts to car parks help drivers arriving at a town centre. Some signs display the number of parking spaces left.*

▼ *Cyclists need secure places to park their bicycles.*

Special needs

For some people, including people with disabilities and people pushing prams or pushchairs, walking into the precinct is difficult. To help them, there need to be:

- car-parking spaces very close to the precinct;

- wider-than-usual car-parking spaces;

- automatic doors;

- lifts, escalators or ramps;

- dropped kerbs.

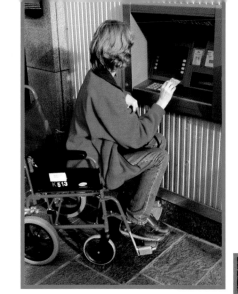

◀ *This cash machine was designed to be easy for a wheelchair user to reach.*

▼ *In car parks, spaces for disabled drivers are positioned close to the pedestrian exit.*

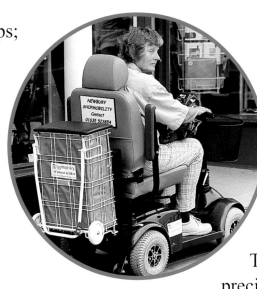

▶ *Some shopping centres have a 'shop-mobility' scheme. Shoppers who would have difficulty walking can borrow a wheelchair or scooter.*

Security

CCTV (closed-circuit television) cameras are often used to help make a pedestrian precinct a safe, secure place. The cameras film what is happening in the precinct and this is watched on TV screens in a control room. Police or security staff may patrol the precinct too.

Pedestrianised areas must be designed so that ambulances, fire engines and police cars could drive in close enough if necessary. Many pedestrianised areas are open to some vehicles (e.g. delivery vehicles) outside normal shopping hours.

For and against

Think about the people who might visit a pedestrian precinct. Choose three or four different types of precinct user and design a table showing the advantages and disadvantages of the precinct for each one.

Some local effects of pedestrianisation

Turning a high street into a pedestrian precinct would have some negative effects on the local environment. People need to decide whether, for their town, these bad effects would be greater or smaller than the benefits of a precinct.

Building work

The work of building the precinct would take a long time. During this time people would have to cope with noise, dust and restricted access to the shops. The town centre could become a mass of road works and building sites.

Road works

Look for boards showing that road works are about to start or are happening at the moment. Notice the start and finish dates on the boards. Do the road works always finish when they are supposed to?

Hertfordshire Highways
Hertfordshire

FOOTWAY REPAIRS

WORK TO START W/C
08- 11 -04
FOR 02 WEEKS
01923 471320

Keswick Town centre Enhancement works
Work starts 19th July 04 until 28th Feb 05

Businesses open as usual

▶ *Shopkeepers say that road works in a town centre are bad for business, because fewer customers come shopping.*

Diverted traffic

Traffic that used to travel through the high street would need to be diverted, so some roads would become busier than before. New routes need careful planning, especially for buses, as bus stops also need to be relocated.

Drivers who could no longer travel through the high street may follow diversion signs or find their own short cuts. These generally take them through smaller, residential side roads. So, although the high street has become a safer place, narrower side roads could become more dangerous as more and bigger vehicles use them instead.

▶ *New problems may be caused by traffic in side streets.*

Think about some of the dangers and ways of trying to reduce them. For example:

- *Problem*: speeding vehicles where children may be playing. *Solution*: traffic-calming measures, such as speed bumps.

- *Problem*: parked cars and traffic making it difficult for emergency vehicles to get through. *Solution*: yellow lines – but then what happens to residents who want to park outside their home?

- *Problem*: parked cars that do not belong to residents. *Solution*: residents' parking permits.

Car parks

Work would be needed to improve car parks and possibly to alter their entrances and exits, for drivers and pedestrians. In some places a park-and-ride scheme can reduce town-centre parking. Large car parks are built on the outskirts of town and special buses or trains are provided from there to the town centre.

◀ *Norwich has several car parks in the city centre, but it costs more to park there than to use the park-and-ride.*

Diverting through traffic

If a high street is pedestrianised, through traffic must find a different route through the town or village. We have thought about some problems that arise with increased traffic in side roads. A solution is to take all through traffic around the perimeter of the town or village, on a ring road or a bypass. You can see a ring road and a bypass on the map on page 23.

A ring road

A ring road is made up of existing, wider roads. Generally, making these into a ring road needs only some road improvements, including new signposting, better pedestrian crossing points and, perhaps, some new roundabouts. People living in these roads may object to the changes and protest about:

- noise pollution both during the alterations and after, when more traffic is passing their homes;
- danger to their children from increased traffic;
- damage to homes by vibrations from traffic.

▲ A ring road takes traffic around a town instead of through the centre. See if you can find this ring road in a road atlas.

▶ When the houses in this main road were built, there was much less traffic than there is today.

A bypass

Building a bypass or relief road is a huge project, as it means building a completely new road outside the town. Local people might object to and protest about:

- destruction of a large area of countryside and wildlife habitats;

- noise pollution;

- loss of passing trade for shopkeepers and other businesses in the town centre;

- the building of out-of-town shopping centres on the bypass and how this would change the character of the town centre;

- cost: who pays for all this work? Council tax and income tax.

▲ A bypass is a main road designed especially to take through traffic around the edge of a town.

▲ This aerial view shows a shopping centre on the outskirts of Sheffield.

Field trip

Make a field trip with an adult to the most likely site for a bypass near your town and see how many plants and animals you find there, for example in one square metre. Present your findings as a bar chart, with a bar to represent each species.

Coming to a decision

Should your high street be closed to traffic? Or are there other changes you would make? To come to a decision about how to improve the high street, you need to gather all the suggestions, comments and data and discuss the advantages and disadvantages of each proposal.

▼ *Who could you interview to find out their opinions on improving your high street?*

You should consider the needs of:

- pedestrians (all groups)
- motorists
- shopkeepers
- delivery people
- emergency services
- local residents
- the local environment.

A class debate

Have a class debate on the *motion*, 'Our High Street should be closed to traffic'. Divide into groups representing each of the groups listed above. Before the debate each group should:

- Prepare a list of advantages and disadvantages of closing the high street to traffic.

- Make a transparency sheet for the overhead projector or a programme for an interactive whiteboard. Keep your points short and to the point.

At the end, have a class vote on the motion and carefully record the results.

These proposals for improvements were displayed on boards in the town centre.

- Then the planning officers present their findings to the Planning Committee. Their advice is not always followed and there can be a long period, perhaps several months, when plans are altered and displayed again. Local newspapers report on the progress of the planning application.

For large projects such as bypasses, other agencies may be involved including:

- The Campaign to Protect Rural England;
- The Environment Agency;
- English Heritage;
- Central Government, with the Secretary of State making the final decision.

How the planning process works

If there are plans for changes in your high street, you might be able to visit an exhibition of the plans. Usually they are displayed in town or village halls or libraries.

Plans for proposed changes must go through several stages before they are either accepted or turned down.

- Applications go first to the Local Planning Authority.
- Plans are displayed for the public to look at and then give their opinions in writing.
- Planning officers look again at the plans and the opinions expressed by the public.

Expressing your ideas

Perhaps you could write a letter to your local planning authority, explaining the work you have been doing and summarising your ideas for improving your high street. Be a good citizen by knowing what is going on in your town or village and expressing your opinions calmly and sensibly.

Glossary

accessible   easy to get to.

bollards   low, strong, wooden or metal posts originally and still used for mooring boats or ships.

bus lane   a section or lane on a road which is meant only for buses.

central refuges   raised areas in the middle of roads, where pedestrians can stand when crossing.

chain stores   shops which have branches in many different places.

citizen   an inhabitant of a city, town or district.

community   the people who live and work in a particular place.

council   the group of people who are elected by local people to run their town or village.

council tax   money paid by each household in a town or village to their local council. It is used by the council to pay for local services such as libraries, street cleaning and school crossing patrols.

decibel   a unit for measuring the intensity of sound.

diverted   directed, by special road signs, to use a different route.

fumes   toxic or poisonous vapours.

graffiti   writing or drawings on walls or other surfaces where it is not allowed.

heart disease   a disease which causes the heart to function less efficiently than it should. It can be caused by obesity although there are many other causes.

high street   the main road going through the centre of a town or village.

Highway Code   a book of rules for all road users. These rules are published by the Department for Transport, which is a government department.

income tax   money paid to the government by everyone who goes to work and earns a wage or salary. This money is used by the government to pay for defence of the country (army, air force, navy), schools, hospitals, the police, fire service, road building and many other important things that we need.

landscaped   designed, built and planted with trees, shrubs and flowers to make a pleasing feature. Some landscaped areas include especially nice-smelling or fragrant flowers for visually impaired people who cannot see the colours.

lease   a legal agreement between an owner of a property and a person or business renting that property.

Local Planning Authority   the group at your local council offices which receives and deals with all applications for permission to build a new house, factory, shop or road.

methane hydrates	a frozen mixture of water and swamp gas which is present in huge quantities under our oceans and polar ice sheets.
motion	the subject that is to be debated or discussed and then voted on.
obesity	a condition where a person is seriously overweight.
Ordnance Survey	Britain's national mapping agency, which makes very detailed maps of every area of Great Britain.
outskirts	areas of a town or village away from the centre.
pedestrian precinct	an area in a village/town/city which is closed to traffic except emergency and delivery vehicles (certain times only).
pelican crossing	a pedestrian road-crossing where pedestrians press a button to cause traffic lights to change to red. The word 'pelican' is adapted from PEdestrian LIght CONtrolled.
Planning Committee	the group that examines planning applications and makes the decisions about whether to grant or refuse permission.
planning officers	the staff who prepare the applications and present them to the planning committee.
pollution	contamination or poisoning of the air, rivers, soil, or the sea by harmful substances. For example, traffic pollutes the air with poisonous fumes from exhaust pipes.

public transport	forms of transport such as trains and buses which can carry large numbers of people at one time.
residential areas	those parts of a town or village, away from the high street, where people live.
rural	in the country.
speed bumps	low humps built across a road, designed to slow down traffic. Sometimes they are called 'sleeping policemen'.
tactile	can be identified through the sense of touch.
tourist board	an organisation that gives visitors to a town or city information about events, places to stay and places of interest to visit.
traffic	all the vehicles that travel on the roads, such as cars, buses, lorries, vans, motorbikes, ambulances, fire engines and police cars.
traffic calming	slowing speed of traffic by various methods such as speed bumps and barriers that make a road 'single-lane' in places.
volume of traffic	the amount of traffic in a certain place which can be measured by counting.
yellow lines	lines painted along the side of roads to show parking restrictions. A single yellow line means 'no parking at certain times' (the times are shown on notices nearby). Double yellow lines mean 'no parking at any time'.

For teachers and parents

This book is designed to support and extend the learning objectives of Unit 12 of the QCA Geography Scheme of Work.

Children are encouraged to observe the high street, investigate the issue of traffic management and collect and use evidence to develop an informed opinion. Their explorations help to raise their awareness of the themes of land use and our responsibilities regarding the environment, and the following skills can be encouraged and developed:

- Observing and questioning
- Collecting and recording evidence
- Analysing and communicating
- Using geographical vocabulary
- Undertaking fieldwork
- Using ICT
- Appreciating the quality of an environment
- Understanding similarities and differences between places

Opportunities also arise for cross-curricular work in design, literacy work (including letter writing), maths, local history, RE, citizenship and PSHE.

SUGGESTED FURTHER ACTIVITIES

Pages 4-5 The high street

To extend the work on these pages you might:

Conduct a survey in class about (a) parents who work in the high street; (b) parents who work somewhere else in the town; (c) parents who work out of town. Use computers to make graphs of the results.

Use information from estate agents or from local papers to compare house prices in the town centre with those further out: for example, a one- or two-bedroom flat in the high street with its equivalent in a more residential area.

Ask the children to find out the names of places of worship in or close to their high street and what religion is practised there. You might follow this up with some research into their main beliefs or festivals.

Pages 6-7 Your high street

The fieldwork suggested could be extended by having four or five other groups working on different activities such as:

(1) sketching or doing rubbings (if it's not too busy at the time) of different paved surfaces.

(2) visiting (exterior only) the oldest church in the high street and either photographing or doing quick sketches of different elevations, to be turned into finished artwork at a later stage.

(3) counting restaurants, places of worship, charity shops, pubs, banks, etc so that, back at school, they can use the data to calculate percentages or make a pie chart.

(4) filling in details on a blank map that you have provided of the high street and any side streets: for example, writing in street names or using appropriate symbols to denote banks, post office, churches etc.

Pages 8-9 Traffic and pedestrians

As part of a literacy lesson, do some research into other words in common use which have Latin roots, for example:

- gratitude from the Latin *gratus* meaning grateful
- origin from the Latin *origo* meaning beginning
- spiral from the Latin *spira* meaning a coil
- fact from the Latin *factus* meaning something done
- colour from the Latin *color* meaning tint or hue

Pages 10-11 Traffic problems

Some traffic problems are caused when there are road works. Apart from repairs to the road structure, what other reasons are there for digging up roads? You might want to investigate with the children, 'What is under our roads?' When you see pipes being laid, what colour are the pipes? Can the children find out what the different colours are used for? The systems of sewers, telephone, gas, electricity and water and their history could be an interesting, ongoing topic for children to work on independently at home.

Pages 12-13 Solving traffic problems

The theme of road safety could be expanded here as part of your PSHE programme. There is a very good website at http://www.thinkroadsafety.gov.uk. It has links for children to the hedgehogs site and other links for parents and teachers. At the teachers' site there is a useful set of age-related lesson plans.

Pages 14-15 Transport for the future

After the children have completed the 'Work out the cost' activity, it would be good to compare their findings with the cost of a similar trip made by car. The children might think that the only cost involved would be the cost of petrol, but you could demonstrate the true cost of motoring to include insurance, road fund licence, petrol, depreciation and servicing. You could then use calculators to work out the cost per mile of an average family's motoring and multiply by the mileage from home to the place chosen for the visit.

Before starting this it would be useful to ask the children whose families have cars to find out how many miles their car travels in one year and then, in class, work out the average annual mileage for your class.

Transport museums are interesting to visit to find out more about the history of transport. In some cases, they also look to the future.

London's Transport Museum is at 39 Wellington Street, London WC2E 7BB; www.ltmuseum.co.uk. You can contact their education officer on (020) 7379 6344.

Amongst other things the museum can provide information on how a station works, safety issues and other citizenship-related issues.

http://temp.sfgov.org/sfenvironment/aboutus/school/resources/ has lots of child-friendly information on trees as recyclers of carbon dioxide into oxygen and other sources of the earth's oxygen supplies.

www.foe.co.uk/campaigns/transport has some very good links to climate change, fossil fuels, green energy and renewable energy.

Pages 16-19 A pedestrian precinct

It might be useful here to follow up the idea of health and why the increasing volume of traffic creates dangers to health. On the previous page you may have done some work on trees as oxygenators. Now this could be linked to how our bodies use oxygen via the lungs.

To help with the activity on page 19, and for much more work on local studies, one useful programme on CD Rom for KS2 is Local Studies Version 4 Primary from Soft Teach. This can be found in the R-E-M catalogue: www.r-e-m.co.uk.

Pages 20-21 Making the precinct accessible

Whilst thinking about the difficulties faced by the emergency services, you might invite a member of one of them to come in, as part of your PSHE programme, to talk about difficulties with access and other issues which might be on your agenda at the time.

Pages 22-23 Some local effects of pedestrianisation

It might be useful to think about diverted traffic in your own local context. Using an interactive whiteboard, if possible, display a street map of your high street. Discuss the pros and cons of a variety of diversions and then ask the children to design one which they feel is the best option. The children could use the maps they made above, under pages 6-7, for this activity.

Pages 24-25 Diverting through traffic

As part of the spiritual, moral, social and cultural elements of this scheme of work, encourage the children to talk to their parents and adult friends and relatives about the pros and cons of out-of-town shopping centres. Ask them to consider what effects these developments have on local shopkeepers and on the high street as the heart of the town or village: i.e. the social aspects of shopping locally and meeting and talking to people. For some this will be a large part of their social contact. Consider also those people who cannot easily get to the out-of-town centres.

Another book in this series, LOCAL TRAFFIC – AN ENVIRONMENTAL ISSUE, explores the issue of building a bypass and contains many ideas for activities on this subject.

Pages 26-27 Coming to a decision

Three websites which might be helpful at adult level are:

www.dft.gov.uk This is the Department for Transport site and gives some insights into how the planning applications for major road building projects are handled.

http://www.highways.gov.uk is the site for the Highways Agency, the organisation responsible for construction and maintenance of trunk roads and motorways.

http://www.cpre.org.uk is the site for the Campaign to Protect Rural England and expresses views on a variety of environmental issues.

Index